Love Muffins:
60 Super #Delish Muffin Recipes

RHONDA BELLE

Copyright © 2016 Rhonda Belle

All rights reserved.

ISBN-13: 978-1540362834

ISBN-10: 1540362833

DEDICATION

To Foodies Everywhere...Enjoy & Be Well!

Table of Contents

Love Muffins for Every Day of the Week 8
    ALL-AMERICAN BLUEBERRY MUFFINS 8
    ALMONDY RICE MUFFINS 9
    APPLE CRANBERRY MUFFINS 9
    BANANA BEAUTIFUL MUFFINS 10
    BERRY-NILLA MUFFINS 10
    BROWN SUGAR NUT MUFFINS 11
    CAPPUCCINO MUFFINS 11
    CARROT CAKE MUFFINS 12
    CHEDDAR PEPPER MUFFINS 12
    CHEESY CORN MUFFINS 12
    CHEESY SAUSAGE MUFFINS 13
    CHOCOLATE CHIP MUFFINS 13
    CINNAMON-RAISIN APPLE MUFFIN MIX 14
    COCO-BANANA MUFFINS 14
    CORRINE'S CORNMEAL MUFFINS 15
    CRANBERRY NUT MUFFINS 15
    CREAM CHEESE MUFFINS 15
    DIABETIC BLUEBERRY MUFFINS 16
    GALA DUMPLING MUFFINS 16
    GOOD MORNING MUFFINS 17
    HAPPY HAM-N-CHEESE MUFFINS 17
    NECTARINE YOGURT MUFFINS 18
    NO FAT BANANA MUFFINS 18
    OAT BRAN MUFFINS 19
    OATMEAL MUFFINS 19
    OLD-FASHIONED POTATO MUFFINS 20
    OLIVE MUFFINS 20
    ONION-WALNUT MUFFINS 21
    ORANGE CURRANT MUFFINS 21
    ORANGE MARMALADE MUFFINS 22
    OREO MUFFINS 22
    PARMESAN HERB MUFFINS 23
    PEANUT BUTTER MUFFINS 23

PEAR BERRY MUFFINS	23
PEACHY PECAN MUFFINS	24
PEPPERONI ENGLISH MUFFIN PIZZAS	24
PINA COLADA MUFFINS	25
PINEAPPLE CITRUS MUFFINS	25
POPPIN' FRESH MUFFINS	26
PUMPKIN GINGER MUFFINS	26
QUICKIE MUFFINS	27
RAISIN BRAN MUFFINS	27
RASPBERRY STREUSEL MUFFINS	27
ROCKY ROAD MUFFINS	28
SKINNY CHOCOLATE MUFFINS	29
SOUR CREAM AND CHIVE MUFFINS (microwave)	29
SOY MUFFINS	30
SPICED PUMPKIN MUFFINS	30
SPICY CINNAMON MUFFIN	31
STRAWBERRY PATCH MUFFINS	31
SUGARLESS FRUIT & NUT MUFFINS	32
SUNNY SIDE UP MUFFINS	32
SWEET POTATO MUFFINS	32
TANGARINE MUFFINS	33
TEX-MEX CORN MUFFINS	34
TROPICAL MUFFINS	34
WELL-WISHES MUFFIN	35
WHOLE WHEAT FRUIT MUFFINS	35
WINE-AND-CHEESE-MUFFINS	36
ZESTY ZUCCHINI-PESTO MUFFINS	36
BONUS	37
SNOW MUFFINS	37

ACKNOWLEDGEMENTS

To the love of my life, Johnny.
You are Mommy's greatest inspiration.

To my Mom & Dad (Sunset February 2016)
Love you both…always!

Love Muffins for Every Day of the Week

Muffins are wonderful! From breakfast to lunch to dinner, a warm and tasty muffin loaded with fresh fruit, nuts or even savory meats and cheeses can serve as a quickie meal or complement a larger buffet. Try these 60 #Delish recipes to make your own batches of tasty muffins from scratch. Limited on time? There are also options for incorporating convenient mixes, puddings and other food items for moist, melt-in-your-mouth goodness that take under 30 minutes to make and will win over tasters time and again.

Some items to have on hand:
- Muffin pan(s). The majority of these recipes are for a dozen to a dozen & a half muffins.
- Nonstick baking or cooking spray or muffin cup liners will help ease your tasty treats out of the muffin tin.
- Active baking powder is important for made-from-scratch recipes.
- Opt for applesauce in place of many of the dairy ingredients such as milk and/or butter. It will add a hint of sweetness and help produce a very moist muffin.

Have fun trying things out! Enjoy!

ALL-AMERICAN BLUEBERRY MUFFINS
¼ teaspoon cinnamon
½ teaspoon nutmeg
¾ cup shortening
¾ teaspoon salt
1 ½ cups milk
1 ½ cups sugar
1 quart fresh blueberries
1 teaspoon vanilla
3 cups flour
3 eggs
4 teaspoons baking powder
Nonstick baking or cooking spray
Combine the sugar and shortening until fluffy. Add eggs and beat again. Slowly begin adding the dry ingredients. Add milk and vanilla. Mix in fresh blueberries gently. Pour into pre-sprayed muffin tins. Bake at 350 degrees for 20 - 30 minutes until golden.

ALMONDY RICE MUFFINS
1 ¼ cups water or soymilk
1 tablespoon arrowroot powder
1 tablespoon non-alum baking powder
1 teaspoon almond extract
½ cup ground almond
¼ cup honey
2 cups brown rice flour
2 tablespoons vegetable oil
Nonstick baking or cooking spray

Preheat oven to 350 degrees. Mix dry and liquid ingredients separately, then combine the two and mix thoroughly. Note that your batter will be very thin. Fill pre-sprayed muffin cups 2/3 full and sprinkle tops with almonds. Bake for 25-30 minutes.

APPLE CRANBERRY MUFFINS
¼ cup butter or margarine, melted
¼ cup sugar
¼ cup sugar
½ teaspoon baking soda
½ teaspoon salt
½ teaspoon ground cinnamon
¾ cup milk
¾ cup sweetened applesauce
1 ½ teaspoons baking powder
1 ¾ cups all-purpose flour
1 cup fresh cranberries, coarsely chopped
1 egg
2 teaspoons all-purpose flour

In medium bowl, combine 1 ¾ cups of flour, ¼ cup sugar, baking powder, baking soda and salt. In small bowl, combine egg, milk, applesauce and butter, mix well. Add egg mixture to flour mixture, stirring just until moistened. Batter will be lumpy. In small bowl, toss chopped cranberries with 2 tablespoon flour, fold into batter. Spoon batter into pre-sprayed 2 ½ inch muffin cups. In another small bowl, combine ¼ cup sugar and the cinnamon. Sprinkle over the tops of the muffins. Bake in preheated 400-degree oven for 20-25 minutes or until a wooden pick inserted in center comes out clean. Remove from pan; cool on wire rack.

BANANA BEAUTIFUL MUFFINS
½ cup butter
½ teaspoon salt
½ teaspoon vanilla
1 ½ cups flour
1 cup sugar
1 teaspoon baking soda
2 eggs, beaten
4 bananas, finely crushed
Nonstick baking or cooking spray
Pecans or walnuts (optional)

Preheat oven to 350 degrees and pre-spray muffin tins. Cream together butter and sugar. Add eggs and crushed bananas. Combine well. Sift together flour, soda and salt. Add to creamed mixture. Add vanilla (and nuts if desired). Pour into muffin cups. Bake for 60 minutes or until done.

BERRY-NILLA MUFFINS
¼ teaspoon salt
½ cup milk
½ cup unsalted butter
½ vanilla bean; cut in small pieces
1 cup sugar
2 ½ cups fresh cranberries; coarsely chopped
2 cups all-purpose flour; unbleached
2 large eggs
2 teaspoons baking powder
Nonstick baking or cooking spray

Topping:
2 teaspoons sugar
½ teaspoon grated nutmeg

Preheat oven to 375 degrees and pre-spray muffin pan. Place the vanilla bean and sugar in a blender or food processor and process until the vanilla bean is ground into tiny bits. Using an electric mixer on low speed, cream the vanilla sugar with the butter in a mixing bowl until smooth. Add the eggs one at a time, beating well after each addition. Mix together the flour, baking powder, and salt. Add the dry ingredients to the creamed mixture alternately with the milk, mixing until smooth and fluffy. Fold in cranberries. Divide the batter between the muffin cups, filling each one almost full. Mix together the sugar and nutmeg for the topping, and sprinkle generously over the muffins. Bake until golden brown, about 25 minutes. Serve warm.

BROWN SUGAR NUT MUFFINS

½ cup buttermilk
½ cup chopped walnuts
½ teaspoon baking soda
½ teaspoon salt
¾ cup packed brown sugar
1 ½ cups all-purpose flour
1 cup rhubarb; diced
1 egg; lightly beaten
1 teaspoon vanilla extract
1/3 cup vegetable oil
Nonstick baking or cooking spray
Topping:
¼ cup chopped walnuts
¼ cup packed brown sugar
½ teaspoon cinnamon

In a large mixing bowl, combine flour, brown sugar, baking soda and salt. Combine oil, egg, buttermilk, and vanilla; stir into dry ingredients just until moistened. Fold in rhubarb and walnuts. Fill pre-greased muffins cups. Combine topping ingredients; sprinkle over muffins. Bake at 3750 degrees for 20-25 minutes or until muffins test done.

CAPPUCCINO MUFFINS

¼ cup brown sugar
½ cup cocoa powder
½ teaspoon salt
¾ cup bittersweet chocolate; finely chopped
¾ cup cake flour
1 ¼ cups unbleached all-purpose flour
1 cup half and half
1 cup sour cream
1 tablespoon baking powder
1 tablespoon finely ground coffee
2 whole eggs
6 tablespoons soft butter
Nonstick baking or cooking spray
Zest of two oranges; minced

Preheat oven to 350 degrees. Sift together the dry ingredients. Mix the butter, sour cream, half and half and eggs until smooth. Fold in the dry ingredients, orange zest and chocolate, until just moistened. Fill pre-greased muffin cups and bake until tops are firm, approximately 15 minutes.

CARROT CAKE MUFFINS
1 ¼ cups whole wheat flour
1 cup wheat bran
1 cup soymilk
1 teaspoon baking soda
1 teaspoon vanilla
1 teaspoon cinnamon
¼ cup oil
1/3 cup sorghum
1/3 cup carrots; shredded
1/3 cup apple, finely chopped
Nonstick baking or cooking spray
Preheat the oven to 400 degrees. Combine flours, bran, baking soda and cinnamon. In another bowl, mix together oil, sorghum, soymilk and vanilla. Combine wet and dry ingredients; mix well. Stir in carrots and apple. Fill greased and floured muffin tins ½ full, and bake for 25 minutes.

CHEDDAR PEPPER MUFFINS
½ teaspoon salt
1 ½ teaspoons freshly ground pepper
1 cup buttermilk
1 cup cheddar cheese; sharp, grated
1 egg; beaten
1 tablespoon baking powder
1 tablespoon sugar
1/3 cup butter; melted
2 cups flour
Nonstick baking or cooking spray
Combine the flour, baking powder, salt, pepper, sugar, and cheese. Mix the buttermilk, beaten egg, and melted butter. Add to the dry ingredients. Stir just long enough to combine. Pour into greased muffin tins and bake in a preheated 400 F oven about 20-25 minutes.

CHEESY CORN MUFFINS
½ cup whole wheat pastry flour
½ teaspoon baking soda
½ teaspoon fresh black pepper
1 cup grated cheddar cheese
1 tablespoons honey
1 tablespoons oil
1 teaspoon baking powder
2 cups buttermilk

2 cups cornmeal
2 eggs beaten
Nonstick baking or cooking spray
Mix all dry ingredients together. Blend in the cheese. In another bowl whisk the wet ingredients together. Make a well in the dry mix and quickly stir in the liquids. Spoon into greased muffin cups. Bake at 375 degrees for 20 to 25 minutes or tested done.

CHEESY SAUSAGE MUFFINS
¼ cup chopped green onions
¼ pound ground pork sausage, cooked and drained
½ cup (2 ounces) shredded cheddar cheese
1 (3-ounce) package cream cheese cut in small pieces
1 cup biscuit mix
2 eggs, beaten lightly
2/3 cup milk
Nonstick baking or cooking spray
Combine sausage, cheeses, onions, and biscuit mix in a large bowl. Make well in the center of the mixture. Combine eggs and milk, and add to sausage mixture, stirring just until moistened. Spoon into a pre-greased muffin pan. Bake at 350 degrees for 35-40 minutes. Remove from pan immediately.

CHOCOLATE CHIP MUFFINS
¼ teaspoon salt
½ cup white sugar
1 ½ cup all-purpose flour
1 cup chocolate chips
1 cup milk
1 egg
1/3 cup melted butter
3 teaspoons baking powder
Nonstick baking or cooking spray
Preheat oven 375 degrees. Mix together dry ingredients, then add liquid ingredients. Pour into pre-sprayed muffin pans. Add chocolate chips last. Do not over stir. Bake for 25 minutes or until done.

CINNAMON-RAISIN APPLE MUFFIN MIX
¼ teaspoon salt
½ cup apple sauce
½ cup raisins
½ teaspoon baking soda
1 cup apple juice
1 teaspoon baking powder
1 teaspoon ground cinnamon
2 cups whole-wheat pastry flour or unbleached flour
2 tablespoons oil
Nonstick baking or cooking spray

Preheat oven to 350 degrees and prepare muffin pan with cooking spray and flour. Mix together 1 cup apple juice, ½ cup apple sauce and 2 tablespoons vegetable oil. Add dry ingredients and raisins and stir until just combined. Spoon into lightly oiled muffin tins, and bake for 20 to 25 minutes, or until done.

COCO-BANANA MUFFINS
¼ egg substitute or 1 egg
½ teaspoon salt
¾ cup milk
1 ½ cups all bran cereal
1 cup flour
1 large banana, mashed
1/3 cup sugar
2 tablespoons cocoa powder
2 tablespoons oil
2 teaspoons baking powder
Nonstick baking or cooking spray

Preheat oven to 400 degrees and pre-spray muffin pan. In a medium bowl, stir together flour, baking powder, salt, cocoa powder and sugar. Combine cereal and milk in large bowl and let stand 2 minutes, or until cereal softens. Add egg or substitute and oil to cereal. Beat well. Stir in bananas. Add flour mix, stirring only once until combined and evenly moist. Spoon batter in muffin cups. Bake for 25 minutes or until muffins are lightly browned.

CORRINE'S CORNMEAL MUFFINS
½ teaspoon salt
¾ teaspoon baking soda
1 ½ cups buttermilk
1 ½ tablespoon butter
1 ½ tablespoon vegetable shortening
1 egg
2 cups cornmeal, sifted
Preheat oven to 400 degrees and grease muffin tins with vegetable oil or nonstick baking spray. Sift cornmeal, soda, and salt into a mixing bowl. Beat egg with buttermilk. Heat shortening with butter until melted. Next, add to egg and buttermilk and blend. Add to dry ingredients all at once and stir just enough to give the mixture a rough appearance. *Add additional buttermilk if mixture seems too dry.* Pour into hot muffin pans and bake about 20 minutes, or until lightly browned. Serve hot butter or jelly for an amazing taste.

CRANBERRY NUT MUFFINS
¾ cup packed brown sugar
1 cup chopped pecans
1 cup cranberries, coarsely
1/3 cup vegetable oil
2 cups flour
2 eggs
2 teaspoons baking powder
2/3 cup orange juice
Nonstick baking or cooking spray
Prepare muffin pan with cooking spray and flour. In a large bowl, combine flour, brown sugar, and baking powder. In another bowl, beat eggs. Add orange juice and oil; stir into the dry ingredients just until moistened (batter will be lumpy). Fold in cranberries and pecans. Spoon into pre-sprayed muffin tins. Bake at 375 degrees for 20 minutes or until golden brown. Remove from pan to cool on a wire rack.

CREAM CHEESE MUFFINS
¼ cup vegetable oil
¼ teaspoon ground nutmeg
½ cup canned pumpkin
½ cup milk
½ teaspoon salt
1 ¼ teaspoons ground cinnamon
1 ½ cups all-purpose flour
1/3 cup sugar
2 eggs; slightly beaten

3 teaspoons baking powder
Nonstick baking or cooking spray
<u>Cream Cheese Filling:</u>
1 tablespoon milk
1 tablespoon sugar
1 (3-ounce) package of cream cheese

Preheat oven to 400 degrees and pre-spray muffin pan. Combine dry ingredients, mixing until smooth. Set aside. Mix eggs, pumpkin, milk and oil. Stir in remaining ingredients until flour is moistened. Fill muffin cups 2/3 full. Divide cream cheese filling among muffins, about 1 teaspoon for each muffin. Place filling on top of each muffin and swirl into batter with knife. Bake 20-22 minutes or until done.

DIABETIC BLUEBERRY MUFFINS

¼ cup vegetable oil
¼ teaspoon allspice
¼ teaspoon cinnamon
½ teaspoon salt
¾ cup concentrated apple juice
1 ¾ cups flour
1 cup fresh or frozen blueberries
1 tablespoon baking powder
1 tablespoon grated lemon rind
2 eggs; beaten (or four egg whites)
Nonstick baking or cooking spray

For a sweeter muffin add 1 or 2 packets of Sweet and Low.

Sift dry ingredients together. Combine beaten eggs, oil, apple juice and rind. Add to dry ingredients and fold in blueberries. Fill well-greased muffin tins. Bake at 375 degrees for 20 to 25 minutes.

GALA DUMPLING MUFFINS

¼ cup oil
¼ teaspoon ground cardamom
¼ teaspoon ground mace
½ teaspoon ground cinnamon
¾ cup milk
1 cup sugar
1 tablespoon baking powder
1 teaspoon salt
1/8 teaspoon ground cloves
2 cups flour
2 eggs
2 gala apples; peeled, cored and cut into slices

4 tablespoons butter or margarine, melted
Nonstick baking or cooking spray
Preheat the oven to 350 degrees. Pre-spray muffin tins. Sift together the flour, sugar, baking powder, salt, cinnamon, mace, cardamom and cloves. Make a well in the center of the flour mixture. By hand, mix in the oil, butter, eggs and milk. Then fold in the sliced apples. Spoon the batter into the prepared muffin pan. Bake in the preheated oven for 30 to 35 minutes or until done.

GOOD MORNING MUFFINS
½ cup flaked coconut
½ cup milk
½ cup raisins
½ cup sliced almonds
½ cup vegetable oil
½ teaspoon salt
¾ cup sugar
1 ½ teaspoons ground cinnamon
1 ½ teaspoons vanilla extract
2 cups all-purpose flour
2 cups carrots; grated
2 cups peeled apples; chopped
2 teaspoons baking soda
3 eggs
Nonstick baking or cooking spray
In a large bowl, combine flour, sugar, baking soda, cinnamon and salt. In another bowl, beat eggs; add oil, milk and vanilla. Mix well, stirring in dry ingredients just until moistened. Fold in the remaining ingredients. Fill greased of paper lined muffin cups ¾ full. Pour into pre-sprayed muffin pan and bake at 375 degrees for 20-25 minutes or until muffins test done.

HAPPY HAM-N-CHEESE MUFFINS
¼ cup vegetable oil
¼ teaspoon salt
½ cup (2-ounces) shredded Swiss cheese
½ teaspoon Worcestershire sauce
¾ teaspoon spicy brown mustard
1 ¾ cups all-purpose flour
1 cup milk
1 egg, beaten lightly
1 tablespoon light brown sugar
1/3 cup finely chopped cooked ham
1/3 cup rye flour
2 teaspoons baking powder

3 drops favorite hot sauce
Nonstick baking or cooking spray

Combine flours, baking powder, salt and sugar in a large bowl. Stir in ham and cheese. Make a well in center of mixture. Combine egg and other ingredients in separate bowl. Add to dry ingredients, stirring just until moistened. Spoon into pre-greased muffin pan. Bake at 400 degrees for 22-25 minutes.

NECTARINE YOGURT MUFFINS
¼ cup butter or margarine; melted
¼ cup sliced almonds
½ cup brown sugar; packed
½ teaspoon salt
½ teaspoon baking soda
1 egg
1 nectarine, chopped
1 peeled peach
2 cups all-purpose flour
2 teaspoons baking powder
8 ounces vanilla yogurt
Nonstick baking or cooking spray

Preheat oven to 400 degrees and prepare muffin pan with cooking spray and flour. In a large bowl, combine the flour, brown sugar, baking powder, baking soda and salt. In a small bowl, combine the yogurt, margarine and egg; blend well. Add to the dry ingredients; stir just until the dry ingredients are moistened. The batter will be very thick. Stir in the nectarine. Fill the muffin cups and sprinkle the almonds over the batter. Bake for 15 to 22 minutes, or until golden brown.

NO FAT BANANA MUFFINS
¼ cup sugar
½ teaspoon baking soda
½ teaspoon cinnamon
½ teaspoon salt; optional
1 ½ cups flour
1/3 cup corn syrup
2 egg whites
2 large bananas; ripe, mashed
2 teaspoons baking powder
2/3 cup skim milk

Spray muffin cups with cooking spray. In medium bowl combine flour, sugar, baking powder, baking soda, salt and cinnamon. In large bowl, using a fork or wire whisk, beat egg whites lightly. Stir in mashed

Bananas, milk and corn syrup. Add flour mixture; stir until well blended. Spoon into prepared muffin cups. Bake at 400 degrees for 22 to 25 minutes or until firm to touch. Cool in pan 5 minutes.

OAT BRAN MUFFINS
¼ cup chopped nuts of your choice
¼ cup honey
¼ cup raisins
1 ¼ cups water
1 tablespoon baking powder
2 ¼ cups oat bran or oatmeal
2 eggs
2 tablespoons olive oil
Nonstick baking or cooking spray
Preheat oven to 425 degrees and prepare muffin pan with cooking spray and flour. Put dry ingredients, raisins and nuts in mixing bowl. Put egg whites, olive oil, honey and water in a blender and mix lightly. Add this mixture to dry ingredients and stir until moistened. Put paper liners in muffin pan and fill about half full. Pour into muffin pan. Bake at 425 degrees for 15 - 17 minutes.

OATMEAL MUFFINS
½ cup packed brown sugar
½ teaspoon baking soda
1 cup butter/sour milk
1 cup quick-cooking oats
1 cup unbleached flour, sifted
1 large egg
1 teaspoon baking powder
1 teaspoon salt
1/3 cups butter or regular margarine
Nonstick baking or cooking spray
Combine oats and butter/sour milk in small bowl. Mix well and let stand for 1 hour. Sift together flour, baking powder, baking soda and salt; set aside. Cream together butter and brown sugar in mixing bowl, using electric mixer at medium speed. Add egg; beat until light and fluffy. Add dry ingredients, blending well after each addition. Spoon batter into pre-greased muffin-pan cups. Bake in 400-degree oven for 20 minutes or until golden brown. Serve hot with homemade jam or preserves.

OLD-FASHIONED POTATO MUFFINS
¼ cup melted butter
¼ teaspoon nutmeg
½ teaspoon baking soda
1 ½ cups buttermilk
1 cup cold, mashed potatoes, about 1 large potato; cooked, mashed and cooled
1 egg
1 teaspoon salt
2 cup all-purpose flour
2 tablespoons granulated sugar
3 teaspoons baking powder
Nonstick baking or cooking spray

Preheat oven to 400 degrees and pre-grease a muffin pan. Measure flour, sugar, baking powder, baking soda, salt and nutmeg into a large mixing bowl. Stir with a fork until mixed, then make a well in center. In a small bowl, beat egg, then gradually stir in mashed potatoes, buttermilk, and butter. Mixture may not be smooth. Then, pour into flour mixture, stirring just until combined. Spoon batter into muffin cups. Bake in center of 400-degree oven until golden and a cake tester inserted into center of a muffin comes out clean, about 20 to 25 minutes. Turn muffins out onto a cooling rack. Serve warm. *Muffins are best the day they are made. To store, seal tightly and freeze.*

OLIVE MUFFINS
1 ½ cups olive oil, plus additional
1 cup grated onion
2 cups chopped pitted black olives
2 tablespoons double action baking powder
2 teaspoons sugar
3 teaspoons chopped fresh mint or 2 teaspoons
4 cups all-purpose flour
Action baking powder
Crushed dried mint
Nonstick baking or cooking spray

Preheat oven to 350 degrees and prepare muffin pan with cooking spray and flour. Rinse olives and drain. Dry on paper towels. Combine all ingredients, adding baking powder last. Bake for 40 to 45 minutes, or until golden and serve warm.

ONION-WALNUT MUFFINS
½ pound unsalted butter, melted
¾ cup sugar
1 tablespoon baking powder
1 tablespoon kosher salt
3 cups all-purpose flour
3 cups walnuts, coarsely chopped
4 extra-large eggs, lightly beaten
4 medium onions; peel/ quartered
Nonstick baking or cooking spray

Preheat the oven to 425 degrees and prepare muffin pan with cooking spray and flour. In a food processor, pulse the onions until pureed. Transfer 2 cups of the onion puree to a bowl and stir in the cooled melted butter, sugar and eggs. One at a time, stir in the salt, baking powder, walnuts and flour; mix thoroughly.

Spoon the batter into the prepared tins and bake for 20 minutes, or until the muffins are brown and a toothpick inserted in the center comes out clean.

ORANGE CURRANT MUFFINS
¼ cup honey
¼ cup safflower oil
½ cup dried currants
½ cup ground almonds
½ cup orange juice
½ cup rolled oats; ground
1 cup rice flour
1 tablespoon baking powder
1 tablespoon maple syrup
1 teaspoon baking soda
1 teaspoon grated orange rind
2 eggs
Nonstick baking or cooking spray

Preheat oven to 400 degrees and pre-spray muffin pan. In a large bowl combine rice flour, baking powder, baking soda, and ground oats. In a separate bowl combine honey, maple syrup, and the ¼ cup oil until very smooth. In a blender or food processor, puree almonds and orange juice, then strain. Add almond liquid to honey mixture along with orange rind. Separate eggs. Stir yolks into honey mixture. Beat egg whites until stiff peaks form. Combine dry and wet ingredients, then stir in currants. Fold in egg whites and finally, spoon into prepared muffin cups. Bake until muffins spring back when pressed lightly in center or for about 20 minutes.

ORANGE MARMALADE MUFFINS
½ cup orange marmalade; plus
¾ cup blueberries; -fresh or frozen
¾ cup nonfat plain yogurt
1 ¼ cups whole wheat flour
1 cup oat bran; or wheat bran
1 tablespoon baking powder
1 tablespoon orange marmalade
1 teaspoon vanilla extract
1/3 cup pecans, chopped (optional)
2 egg whites
Nonstick baking or cooking spray

Preheat oven to 350 degrees and prepare muffin pan with cooking spray and flour. Combine the flour, bran and baking powder; stir to mix well. Add the yogurt, marmalade, egg whites and vanilla extract; stir just until the dry ingredients are moistened. Fold in the pecans or blueberries, if desired. Fill the muffin cups 3/4 full with the batter. Bake for about 15 minutes, or just until a toothpick inserted in the center comes out clean. Remove the muffin tin from the oven and allow it to sit for 5 minutes before removing the muffins. Serve warm or at room temperature.

OREO MUFFINS
¼ cup margarine, melted
½ cup sugar
½ teaspoon salt
¾ cup milk
1 ¾ cups all-purpose flour
1 egg
1 tablespoons baking powder
1/3 cup sour cream
Nonstick baking or cooking spray
20 OREO chocolate sandwich cookies, crushed.

In medium bowl, combine flour, sugar, baking powder and salt; set aside. In small bowl, combine milk, sour cream and egg; stir into flour mixture with margarine until just blended. Gently stir in cookies. Spoon batter into muffin-pan cups. Bake at 400 degrees for 20 to 25 minutes or until toothpick inserted in center comes out clean.

PARMESAN HERB MUFFINS

¼ cup butter/margarine, melted
¼ cup grated parmesan cheese
½ cup chopped fresh parsley
½ teaspoon baking soda
½ teaspoon sage leaves, crumbled
1 ¼ cups butter/sour milk
1 ½ teaspoons baking powder
1 large egg
1 teaspoons sugar
2 cups unbleached flour
Nonstick baking or cooking spray

Heat oven to 400 degrees and prepare muffin pan with cooking spray and flour. Lightly spoon flour into measuring cup and level off. In large bowl, combine flour sugar, baking powder, baking soda, sage, parsley and cheese, blend well. Add butter/sour milk, margarine and egg; stir just until dry ingredients are moistened. Fill prepared muffin cups. Bake at 400 degrees for 15 to 20 minutes or until toothpick inserted in center comes out clean. Serve hot.

PEANUT BUTTER MUFFINS

¼ cup milk
1 cup variety baking mix
1 egg
2 tablespoons peanut butter
2 tablespoons sugar
2 tablespoons vegetable oil
Nonstick baking or cooking spray

Prepare muffin pan with cooking spray and flour. Beat all ingredients except baking mix in medium bowl with wire whisk or hand mixer until well blended. Stir in baking mix just until moistened. Fill each cup with scant 1/4 cup batter. Microwave uncovered on high 2 to 4 minutes, rotating ring 1/4 turn every minute, until tops are almost dry and wooden pick inserted in center comes out clean. Serve warm...with jelly if desired.

PEAR BERRY MUFFINS

¾ cup coarsely chopped walnuts
¾ cup buttermilk
1 cups fresh or frozen cranberries; thawed
1 egg
1 large firm pear, peeled; cut into half inch cubes
1 package Pillsbury Apple Cinnamon Quick Bread
3 tablespoons oil
Nonstick baking or cooking spray

Preheat oven to 400 degrees and prepare muffin pan with cooking spray and flour. In large bowl, combine quick bread mix, buttermilk, oil and egg. Stir until mix is moistened. Stir in cranberries, walnuts and pear. Spoon batter into pre-sprayed muffin pan. Bake for 18 to 25 minutes or until golden brown.

PEACHY PECAN MUFFINS
½ cup peach preserves
½ cup sour cream
½ cup sugar
½ teaspoon baking soda
½ teaspoon salt
1 ¾ cups sifted all-purpose flour
1 egg
1 teaspoons baking powder
1 teaspoons vanilla extract
2/3 cups pecans, chopped and toasted
Nonstick baking or cooking spray

Position rack in center of oven, preheat to 400 degrees and prepare muffin pan with cooking spray and flour. Sift flour, sugar, baking powder, baking soda, and salt into large bowl. Whisk sour cream, preserves, egg and vanilla to blend in medium bowl. Add sour cream mixture and pecans to dry ingredients and stir just until combined; do not over mix. Pour into muffin cups. Bake until tester inserted into center of muffins comes out clean, about 20 minutes.

PEPPERONI ENGLISH MUFFIN PIZZAS
½ cup tomato sauce
½ teaspoon Italian seasoning
4 English muffins
4-ounces mozzarella cheese, grated
4-ounces pepperoni, finely chopped
Nonstick baking or cooking spray

Split English muffins in half; toast them. Turn on the oven broiler. Lightly coat a baking sheet with cooking spray. Place English muffin halves, cut side up, on baking sheet. Spread each muffin half with a little tomato sauce. Sprinkle with a pinch of Italian seasoning. Top each muffin half with mozzarella and pepperoni. Broil the pizzas about 6 inches from the source of heat for 3 to 4 minutes or until lightly browned.

PINA COLADA MUFFINS

¼ cup butter, melted
½ cup granulated sugar
½ cup light sour cream
1 ½ cups all-purpose flour
1 (14- ounce) can crushed pineapple, drained
1 egg
1/2 teaspoon baking soda
1/2 teaspoon salt
12 maraschino cherries, finely chopped (optional)
2 teaspoons rum extract or ¼ cup rum
2 teaspoons baking powder
3/4 cups shredded coconut
Nonstick baking or cooking spray

Preheat oven to 400 degrees and prepare muffin pan with cooking spray and flour. In a medium-sized mixing bowl, in a small bowl, beat egg lightly, then stir in drained pineapple, sour cream, sugar, butter and rum extract. Measure flour, baking powder, baking soda, and salt into a large mixing bowl. Stir with a fork until mixed, then make a well in center. Mixture may not be smooth. Then, pour in pineapple mixture, stirring just until combined. Fold in coconut and cherries. Immediately spoon batter into muffin cups. Bake in center of 400-degree oven until a pale golden color, and a cake tester inserted into center of a muffin comes out clean, about 25 to 30 minutes.

PINEAPPLE CITRUS MUFFINS

¼ cup sugar
½ cup brown sugar, packed
½ teaspoon salt
1 ¾ ounces pineapple, crushed & drained
1 cup skim milk
1 egg; large; beaten
1 teaspoon lemon peel, grated
1/8 teaspoon nutmeg
1/8 teaspoon nutmeg, ground
2 cups whole wheat flour
3 tablespoons margarine, melted
3 tablespoons vegetable oil
3 teaspoons baking powder
8 maraschino cherries, halved
Nonstick baking or cooking spray

Combine the brown sugar, lemon peel, the first 1/8 teaspoon nutmeg and the melted shortening. Prepare muffin pan with cooking spray and flour. Place a spoonful of the drained canned pineapple and a cherry half in the bottom of each cup. In a mixing bowl, combine the flour, sugar, and baking powder, salt and remaining nutmeg. Make a well in the center of the mixture and add the egg, milk and oil which have been blended well before adding. Add all at once to the dry ingredients and stir until just moistened and no streaks remain. Spoon into the prepared muffin cups and bake in a 375-degree oven for 18 to 20 minutes or until done.

POPPIN' FRESH MUFFINS
1 ¾ (13-ounce can) cups evaporated milk
1 teaspoon almond extract
1 teaspoon vanilla
½ cup poppy seeds
½ teaspoon salt
¼ cup milk
2 cups sugar
2 cups vegetable oil
3 ½ teaspoons baking powder
4 cups flour
4 large eggs
Nonstick baking or cooking spray
Preheat the oven to 325 degrees. Line muffin cups with paper liners or spray with nonstick oil. In a large mixing bowl, beat together the eggs, sugar, evaporated milk, milk and vegetable oil. Sift together baking powder, salt and flour. Gradually add the flour mixture to the egg mixture, beating until well combined. Add the extracts and poppy seeds, stirring only until well combined. Pour batter into the prepared muffin cups. Bake for 25-30 minutes or until a toothpick inserted into the center of a muffin comes out clean.

PUMPKIN GINGER MUFFINS
½ cup apple juice at room temperature
1 ½ cups mashed pumpkin
1 ½ cups unbleached flour
1 teaspoon nutmeg
1 teaspoon salt
2 cups brown sugar, packed
2 egg whites, whipped
2 teaspoons baking powder
2 teaspoons baking soda
4 ½ teaspoons ginger
5 tablespoons applesauce
Nonstick baking or cooking spray
Preheat oven at 350 degrees. Prepare muffin tins with cooking spray and flour. In a mixing bowl, combine pumpkin, applesauce, egg whites, and juice. In

another mixing bowl, combine sugar, flour, baking soda, baking powder, salt, ginger, and nutmeg. Mix wet ingredients with dry ingredients just until moistened. Use an ice cream scoop to fill muffin tins two thirds full. Bake 25 minutes.

QUICKIE MUFFINS
1 cup oil
1 quart buttermilk biscuit mix
2 teaspoons salt
3 cups sugar
4 eggs
5 cups flour
5 teaspoons baking soda
Nonstick baking or cooking spray
One 15-ounce box raisin bran or any selected bran flakes
Mix all ingredients in a large bowl at medium speed. Pour into pre-sprayed muffin pan and bake in a muffin pan at 400 degrees for 15-20 minutes.

RAISIN BRAN MUFFINS
¼ cup melted butter
¼ teaspoon salt
½ cup honey
½ teaspoon cinnamon
1 ½ tablespoons baking powder
1 1/3 cups all-purpose flour
1 1/3 cups milk
2 eggs; well beaten
3 cups raisin bran
Nonstick baking or cooking spray
Sift together flour, baking powder, salt, and cinnamon. Pour milk over raisin bran, stir, and let stand 5 minutes. Stir in eggs, melted butter, and honey. Add dry ingredients and stir just until moistened. Spoon batter into pre-greased muffin pans. Bake at 400 degrees for 20 minutes or until a toothpick inserted in a muffin comes out clean.

RASPBERRY STREUSEL MUFFINS
¼ cup brown sugar, packed
¼ cup sugar
¼ teaspoon salt
½ cup margarine, melted
½ cup skim milk
1 ¼ cups raspberries, fresh or frozen
1 ½ cups whole wheat flour

1 large egg, lightly beaten
1 teaspoon lemon zest, grated
1 teaspoons cinnamon
<u>Topping:</u>
¼ cup whole wheat flour
½ cup brown sugar; packed
½ cup pecans; chopped
1 teaspoons cinnamon
1 teaspoons lemon zest
2 tablespoons margarine
Nonstick baking or cooking spray

Sift the flour, sugar, brown sugar, baking powder, salt and cinnamon together in a medium bowl. Make a well in the center. Place the egg, margarine and milk in the well. Stir with a wooden spoon just until the ingredients are combined. Quickly stir in the raspberries and lemon zest. Fill muffin tins, which have been sprayed with a non-stick coating, three fourths full. Make the topping by combining the pecans, brown sugar, flour, cinnamon, and lemon zest together. Pour in the melted margarine and stir to combine into crumbs. Sprinkle evenly over the tops of each muffin. Bake in a 350-degree oven for 20 to 25 minutes.

ROCKY ROAD MUFFINS

¼ cup light corn syrup
¼ teaspoon salt
½ cup brown sugar
¾ cup sour cream
1 ¼ teaspoons vanilla
1 ½ cups flour
1 egg
1 ounces unsweetened chocolate
1 teaspoon baking soda
2/3 cup chopped walnuts (or nuts of your choice)
2/3 cup mini-marshmallows
4 ounces semi-sweet chocolate pieces
Nonstick baking or cooking spray

Melt chocolate in a double boiler. Whisk liquid ingredients in a small bowl. Put remaining ingredients in a large bowl and mix (except nuts and marshmallows) Add melted chocolate to liquid mixture. Pour this into dry mixture blending only to combine. Fold in nuts and marshmallows. Batter will be lumpy. Spoon into pre-sprayed muffin cups. Bake at 400 degrees for 18 to 20 minutes until tested done.

SKINNY CHOCOLATE MUFFINS

¼ cup cocoa powder
½ teaspoon salt
½ teaspoon vanilla extract
¾ cup granulated sugar
1 ½ cups all-purpose flour
1 teaspoon baking soda
2 teaspoons baking powder
2/3 cup vanilla low-fat yogurt
2/3 cup skim milk
Nonstick baking or cooking spray
Powdered sugar (optional)

Heat oven to 400 degrees and pre-spray muffin pan. In medium bowl, stir together flour, granulated sugar, cocoa, baking powder, baking soda and salt; stir in yogurt, milk and vanilla just until combined. Do not beat. Fill muffin cups 2/3 full with batter. Bake 15-20 minutes or until wooden pick inserted in center comes out clean. Cool slightly in pan on wire rack. Remove from pans. Sprinkle powdered sugar over tops of muffins, if desired.

SOUR CREAM AND CHIVE MUFFINS (microwave)

¼ cup milk
¼ cup sour cream
¼ cup vegetable oil
¼ teaspoon baking soda
¼ teaspoon salt
¾ cup all-purpose flour
¾ teaspoon baking powder
1 egg
2 tablespoons chopped fresh chives
Nonstick baking or cooking spray

Beat sour cream, milk, oil and egg in medium bowl with fork. Stir in remaining ingredients, all at once, just until flour is moistened. Fill each pre-greased muffin cup with batter. Sprinkle with additional chopped fresh chives if desired. Microwave uncovered on high 2 to 4 minutes, rotating ring ¼ turn every minute, until tops are almost dry and wooden pick inserted in center comes out clean. *(Parts of muffins may appear slightly moist but will continue to cook while standing.)*

SOY MUFFINS

¼ cup chopped nuts
¼ cup raisins
1 ½ cups soy flour
1 cup milk
1 pinch salt
1 tablespoon butter or margarine; melted
1 tablespoon grated orange peel
2 eggs, separated
2 teaspoons baking powder
3 tablespoons brown sugar
Nonstick baking or cooking spray

Mix beaten yolks add brown sugar and orange peel and melted butter. Sift and add dry ingredients alternately with the milk. Blend in stiffly beaten whites. Fold in raisins and nuts. Pour into pre-greased muffin pan. Bake at 325 degrees for 35 minutes or until done.

SPICED PUMPKIN MUFFINS

¼ teaspoon ground nutmeg
½ cup canned pumpkin
½ cup chopped pecans (about 2 oz.)
½ cup raisins
½ teaspoon ground cinnamon
¾ cup vegetable oil
1 ½ cups self-rising flour
1 cup sugar
2 large eggs
Nonstick baking or cooking spray

Preheat oven to 350 degrees and prepare muffin pan with cooking spray and flour. Place raisins in small bowl. Pour enough boiling water over to cover. Let stand 5 minutes. Drain raisins. Mix flour, sugar, cinnamon and nutmeg in large bowl. Add oil, pumpkin and eggs; mix just until combined. Mix in raisins and chopped pecans. Pour into prepared muffin cups. Bake until tester inserted in center of muffins comes out clean, about 25 minutes.

SPICY CINNAMON MUFFIN

¼ teaspoon salt
¼ teaspoon white pepper
½ teaspoon cloves
½ cup granulated sugar
1 ¾ cups flour
1 cups skim milk; at room temperature
1 egg white; whipped
1 teaspoons cinnamon
1 teaspoons orange peel
1/3 cup margarine, softened at room temperature
2 teaspoons baking powder
Nonstick baking or cooking spray

Glaze:
½ cups powdered sugar
1 tablespoon lemon juice
60 cinnamon candies

Preheat oven at 350 degrees and prepare muffin pan with cooking spray and flour. In mixing bowl, combine flour, sugar, baking powder, cinnamon, salt, cloves, and pepper. In another mixing bowl, combine orange peel, egg white, milk, and margarine. Mix wet ingredients with dry ingredients just until moistened. Use an ice cream scoop to fill muffin tins 2/3 full. To prepare glaze, combine powdered sugar and lemon juice. Bake for 20 minutes. While still warm, spread glaze on muffins. Press 5 candies into glaze.

STRAWBERRY PATCH MUFFINS

½ teaspoon salt
¾ teaspoon ground cinnamon
1 ¼ teaspoons vanilla extract
1 ½ cups fresh strawberries; sliced
1 ½ tablespoons sugar
1 cup nonfat buttermilk
1 teaspoon baking soda
1 whole egg white, lightly beaten
1 whole egg. lightly beaten
1/3 cup margarine; melted
2 ½ cups all-purpose flour
Nonstick baking or cooking spray
2/3 cup sugar

Combine flour, 2/3 cup sugar, soda and cinnamon in a large bowl, and stir well. Add fresh strawberries; stir well, and make a well in center of mixture. Combine buttermilk and margarine, vanilla, sugar, and eggs. Stir well. Add to dry ingredients, stirring just until moistened. Pour into prepared muffin pans.

Sprinkle 1 ½ tablespoons sugar evenly over muffins. Bake at 350 degrees for 25 minutes or until done.

SUGARLESS FRUIT & NUT MUFFINS
¼ teaspoon salt
½ cup chopped nuts, optional
½ cup chopped prunes
½ cup margarine
½ cup raisins
1 cup chopped dates
1 cup flour
1 cup water
1 teaspoon baking soda
1 teaspoon vanilla
2 eggs, beaten
Nonstick baking or cooking spray

In a saucepan, combine dates, raisins, prunes and water. Bring to boil and boil 5 minutes. Stir in margarine and salt. Set aside to cool. Add remaining ingredients to fruit; stir just until dry ingredients are moistened. Spoon into greased muffin tins. Bake at 350 degrees for 15 minutes.

SUNNY SIDE UP MUFFINS
½ cup chopped pecans
½ cup orange juice
½ cup orange marmalade
1 large egg, beaten
2 cups biscuit mix
2 tablespoons margarine, melted
2/3 cup sugar
Nonstick baking or cooking spray

Combine egg, sugar, orange juice and margarine in a large bowl. Mix well. Stir in biscuit mix. Mix well. Fill greased muffin tins two-thirds, fill with batter. Bake in a preheated 400-degree oven for 20 to 25 minutes.

SWEET POTATO MUFFINS
¼ cup all-purpose flour
¼ teaspoon salt
½ cup chopped pecans
½ cup firmly packed brown sugar
½ cup veggie oil
½ teaspoon ground cinnamon
1 (17-ounce) can sweet potatoes, drained and mashed
1 ¾ cups all-purpose flour

1 cup dates, chopped
1 cup sugar
1 teaspoon baking soda
2 eggs
Nonstick baking or cooking spray

Combine flour, soda, cinnamon, and salt in a large bowl. Make a well in the center of mixture. Combine eggs and sugars, oil, and sweet potatoes in a bowl. Beat at medium speed with an electric hand mixer until well blended. Add this mixture to dry ingredients and stir just until moistened. Dredge pecans and dates in ¼ cup flour. Fold in muffin mixture. Spoon in pre-greased muffin pan. Bake at 350 degrees for 27-30 minutes. Cool for 5 minutes before removing from pan to wire rack.

TANGARINE MUFFINS

¼ cup butter, melted
½ cup sugar
½ teaspoon salt
1 (8-ounce) carton vanilla yogurt
1 cup diced peeled tangerine
1 egg, lightly beaten
1 tablespoon grated tangerine peel
1 teaspoon baking soda
2 cups flour
2 tablespoons milk
2 teaspoons baking powder
Nonstick baking or cooking spray

In a bowl, combine flour, sugar, baking powder and soda, and salt ingredients. In a small bowl, combine the yogurt, egg, butter and milk until smooth; stir into dry ingredients just until moistened. Stir in tangerine and peel. Fill greased or paper-lined muffin cups two-thirds full.

Bake at 400° for 18-20 minutes. Cool for 5 minutes before removing from pan to wire rack.

TEX-MEX CORN MUFFINS

½ cup finely chopped onion
½ teaspoon baking soda
½ teaspoon salt
1 (2-ounce) jar diced pimento, drained
1 (8 ¾ ounce) can yellow cream-style corn
1 ½ cups yellow cornmeal
1 clove garlic, minced
1 cup (4-ounces) shredded cheddar cheese
1 cup chopped green chills
1 cup milk
2 eggs, beaten lightly
Nonstick baking or cooking spray

Combine cornmeal, soda and salt in a large bowl. Stir in pimento and cheese, onion, chills and garlic. Make a well in the center of the mixture. Combine eggs, milk and corn. Add to dry ingredients, stirring just until moistened. Spoon into prepared muffin pan. Bake at 400 degrees for 30 minutes until golden. Remove from pan immediately.

TROPICAL MUFFINS

¼ cup firmly packed brown sugar
¼ cup vegetable oil
¼ teaspoon salt
½ cup milk
½ teaspoon cinnamon
¾ cup sweetened flaked coconut, toasted lightly
1 ½ teaspoons double-acting baking powder
1 cup all-purpose flour
1 large egg white
6 teaspoons pineapple preserves
Nonstick baking or cooking spray

Prepare muffin pan with cooking spray and flour. Drop 1 heaping teaspoon of the preserves into the bottom of a well-oiled muffin cup. In a bowl, whisk together the brown sugar, the oil, and the egg white until the mixture is smooth and whisk in the milk. In another bowl whisk together the flour, the baking powder, the cinnamon, the salt, and the coconut, add the milk mixture, and stir the batter until it is just combined. Divide the batter among the tins and bake the muffins in the middle of a preheated 400-degree oven for 20 minutes, or until a tester comes out clean. Let the muffins cool for 3 minutes, run a knife around each muffin, and lift each muffin out with a fork, inverting it upside-down onto a rack.

WELL-WISHES MUFFIN
¼ cup firmly packed brown sugar
¼ cup molasses or honey
¼ cup vegetable oil
½ cup raisins, blueberries, chopped dates, apple or nuts.
¾ cup bran cereal
¾ cup whole or chocolate milk
1 cups quick oats, uncooked
1 egg
1 teaspoon baking powder
2/3 cup flour
Salt to taste
Nonstick baking or cooking spray
Combine milk and bran cereal in medium sized bowl. Add egg, oil, molasses and brown sugar; mix well. Add combined remaining ingredients, mixing just until dry ingredients are moistened. Pour into pre-sprayed muffin pan. Bake in preheated 400-degree oven for about 15 minutes.

WHOLE WHEAT FRUIT MUFFINS
¼ teaspoon salt (or less)
½ cup applesauce
1 ¼ cups water
1 large apple or 2 small apples, chopped (about 1 ½ cups)
1 teaspoons cinnamon
2 cups whole wheat flour
2 teaspoons sugar (may use ¼ cup for sweeter muffins)
3 teaspoons baking powder
Nonstick baking or cooking spray
Combine dry ingredients in large mixing bowl. Combine water and applesauce in another bowl. Add apple to dry ingredients and mix to coat apple. Add water mixture to dry ingredients. *Mixture will be somewhat thick.* Spoon mixture into pre-greased muffin pan. Bake at 425 degrees for about 20 minutes or until lightly browned. Sprinkle top with cinnamon if desired.

WINE-AND-CHEESE-MUFFINS
1 cup shredded Swiss; gruyere or cheddar cheese (4 ounces)
1 egg
2 cups variety biscuit mix
2 tablespoons vegetable oil
2 teaspoons chopped fresh or freeze-dried chives
2/3 cup white wine or apple juice
Nonstick baking or cooking spray

Heat oven to 400 degrees and pre-spray muffin tin. Make biscuit mix, wine, oil and egg with fork. Beat well. Stir in remaining ingredients. Divide batter evenly among cups. Bake about 20 minutes or until golden brown.

ZESTY ZUCCHINI-PESTO MUFFINS
½ cup pine nuts
½ teaspoon salt
1 ½ cups unbleached all-purpose flour
1 cup whole wheat flour
1 cup zucchini squash; unpeeled & shredded
1 large egg
1 teaspoon minced garlic
1/3 cup grated Romano cheese; freshly grated
1/3 cup virgin olive oil
2 large egg whites
2/3 cup skim milk
3 tablespoons minced fresh basil
4 teaspoons baking powder
Nonstick baking or cooking spray

Set oven to 425 degrees and pre-spray muffin pan. In a big bowl, sift the flours, baking powder and salt. In a small bowl, whisk together egg, egg whites, milk, and oil until well blended. Add the small bowl's egg mixture to big bowl's flour. Stir in the zucchini, basil, garlic, cheese, and pine nuts. Fill each muffin cup full of batter. Bake until the muffins are golden brown and spring back when touched lightly, about 20 minutes.

BONUS
SNOW MUFFINS

½ cup clean white snow*
½ cup raisins
½ cup white or brown sugar
½ teaspoon grated lemon or orange rind
¾ teaspoon salt
¾ cups milk
2 cups sifted cake & pastry flour
Nonstick baking or cooking spray
3 tablespoons melted butter
3 teaspoons baking powder

Mix dry ingredients in a bowl. Make a well in the center and pour in the milk, butter and grated rind. Stir slightly. Add snow and raisins. Stir only until dry ingredients disappear. Spoon into pre-greased muffin cups. Bake at 400 degrees for 15 to 18 minutes. Serve hot with butter or strawberry preserves.

*Clean frost from a freezer or shaved ice may be used instead of snow.

Thank you for your purchase!
May you enjoy and be well!

ABOUT THE AUTHOR

I am a Tennessee native and a connoisseur of great tastes. My culinary delights are inspired by my Southern roots.

I am from cornbread and cabbage, fried chicken and Kool-Aid soaked lemon slices.

I am from hen houses, persimmon trees and juicy, red tomatoes on the vine.

I am from sunflowers growing wild in summer and homemade ice cream in the winter.

I am from family reunions, blue collar men, happy housewives, and Sunday dinners.

I am from spiritual folks who didn't always get it right, but believed in the power of prayer – and taught it to their kids.

I am from the hottest of hot summers and kids running barefoot and free through thirsty Tennessee grass.

I am from a grandmother who sang gospel that was magic…song drenched air would tumble from her lungs, leap into your spirit and make you feel fantastic things.

I am from hard, heartfelt lessons about living and kitchens full of the perfume of love.

♥♥♥ *This book is from my heart to yours.* ♥♥♥

Find more cookbooks online at http://www.tinyurl.com/sodelishdish.
For freebies & new book announcements, follow @SoDelishDish on social media!

Scan with your smartphone!

Printed in Germany
by Amazon Distribution
GmbH, Leipzig